Pam

D0285119

OTHER COUNTRIES IN THIS SERIES

THE SIMPLE GUIDE TO

FRANCE

CUSTOMS & ETIQUETTE

COVER ILLUSTRATION

Rural landscape typical of what the French sometimes refer to as
La France profonde – 'Deep France'

ABOUT THE AUTHOR

DANIELLE ROBINSON was born and bred in the South of France,
(Toulouse). After teaching French all over England, she now lives in
Yorkshire, where she is honorary visiting Fellow at the University of
Bradford. She is also author of *The Simple Guide to Islam*.

ILLUSTRATED BY
IRENE SANDERSON

THE SIMPLE GUIDE TO
FRANCE

CUSTOMS & ETIQUETTE

Danielle Robinson

GLOBAL BOOKS LTD

Simple Guides • Series 1
CUSTOMS & ETIQUETTE

The Simple Guide to
FRANCE
CUSTOMS & ETIQUETTE

Originally published 1992 as
Simple Etiquette in France

This fully revised second edition first published 1998 by
Global Books Ltd
PO Box 219, Folkestone, Kent CT20 3LZ, England

© Global Books Ltd 1998

ISBN 1–86034–006–7

British Library Cataloguing in Publication Data
A CIP catalogue entry for this book
is available from the British Library.

Distributed in the USA by:
The Talman Co, Inc, New York

Set in Futura 11 on 12 pt by Bookman, Hayes, Middx
Printed and bound in Great Britain by
The Cromwell Press, Broughton Gifford, Wilts.

Contents

For Eileen, my English mother-in-law who has met my quaint 'French' behaviour with unfailing equanimity and affection.

Foreword

France is a fascinating country. You know this already and have now decided to go and see for yourself properly, not just as a hurried tourist shepherded by a travel firm's representative. You may be going there on business, or wondering whether it is at all possible to do business there; or you may be going for the most important business of all, your own business, on whatever quest or dream you wish to pursue. In order to be successful, you will need to interact with the French.

Unless you speak their language perfectly, you will be perceived as a *foreigner* and excuses will therefore be made for your 'odd' behaviour. That does not mean, however, that you should feel or be made to feel an *outsider*.

The aim of this fully revised guide is to bring you up to date with recent developments in French society and to enable you to gain access to a culture and way of life which started flourishing in Gallo-Roman times nearly two thousand years ago and is forever changing as it faces up to the impact of a united Europe and globalization.

This is only a simple introduction to a huge and diverse topic, but the hope is that it will make you feel more at ease with the customs and etiquette of a very varied nation. The wonderful thing is that nobody understands the French perfectly and they seem always to disagree amongst themselves – disparaging their achievements at the same time as they praise them. International experts say that they only do this because they are so interested in themselves. Frustrating? No, fascinating! So take heart and enjoy France.

DANIELLE ROBINSON

1

Introducing France

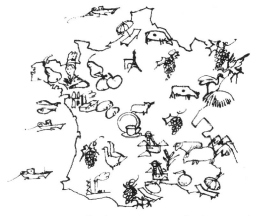

'. . .a great variety of culture, customs and culinary traditions'

Excluding Russia, France is the largest country in Europe (551,602km^2, including Corsica) but with a population of 58 million it is, in fact, one of the least densely populated. There are many large towns and cities but also vast rural areas with very few inhabitants and, in some regions, villages have been abandoned. In recent years, Europeans from more crowded countries such as Germany, Great Britain or the Netherlands have bought these abandoned houses, including many farmhouses, which are often situated in areas of breathtaking beauty.

MAP OF FRANCE

The locals are intrigued with such activity and follow the enthusiastic arrival of removal vans with some amusement, wondering how long the fad will last. Although prices can be much lower than for a similar property in, say, the UK, solicitor's fees (*frais de notaire*) are high. French banks can be helpful in providing French mortgages and also guidelines from their London offices. It is also advisable to make enquiries from the town hall (*mairie*) of your dream village. But beware, too many such dreams have already ended in nightmares.

The shape of France is roughly that of a hexagon and French people very often use this term when they refer to their country. The other term besides '*l'Hexagone*' is '*la France métropolitaine*' or just '*la métropole*' which has nothing to do with *le métro* (the tube, subway), but signals the difference between *la mère patrie* (mother country=fatherland!) and the colonies, or what is left of them in the form of *DOM* or *TOM* (*Départements d'outre mer* and *Territoires d'outre mer*=overseas).

Three of the sides of the hexagon of course can clearly be seen to be coastlines (the Channel, the Atlantic Ocean to the west and the Mediterranean to the south-east), and one side is a mountain range, (the *Pyrénées*; literally 'born of fire') separating France from Spain. Another side is made up of mountains (the Alps and Jura separating France from Italy and Switzerland) and part of the river Rhine, (a border with Germany). The North-East is the only side not to have natural frontiers with its neighbours (Germany, Luxemburg and Belgium).

There is a great diversity of landscape and variations in climate. In the northern and western parts the sea ensures mild winters but the eastern regions have a harsher climate of a more continental nature. On the Mediterranean coast people enjoy very mild winters but the summers can be unbearably hot.

Although France has been a unified and very centralized country for centuries, its regions have retained a great variety of culture, customs and culinary traditions.

For administrative purposes France is divided into 100 *départements* (96 in the *métropole* and 4 DOM) which are grouped into 26 *régions* (22 in *l'Hexagone* and 4 DOM). *Départements* are ordered alphabetically and numbered. These numbers are used as postal codes and as the last two digits of car registration numbers; for example 75 stands for Paris.

Départements were introduced after the 1789 revolution, but when asked where he comes from, a Frenchman will probably use the name of the pre-revolutionary province and proudly declare he was born in Brittany, Normandy or Provence, which are cultural entities. The names immediately conjure up a particular type of landscape, climate, traditions, specialities and way of speaking.

Rivers as well as mountains provide a useful way of quickly situating a town or area since a great many *départements* are named after them. You already know that Paris is **on** the SEINE (river) and **in** the Seine (*département* 75). You may enjoy following the course of the other great rivers (*fleuves*). France has five *fleuves* and a great many lesser *rivières*. You will have heard of the LOIRE, famous for its beautiful Renaissance châteaux and fine light wines. The area is also supposed to have the purest French accent and was certainly the heart of civilization in the sixteenth century.

The RHINE as mentioned above, separates the province of Alsace from the Black Forest in Germany and was for long a bitterly disputed territory. The city of Strasb(o)urg now symbolizes the new era of peace with its European Parliament. The powerful RHÔNE, coming from Switzerland through Lake Geneva changes direction at Lyon and then flows South; Marseille is found on its Mediterranean delta.

The French spelling of these very important cities, second and third after Paris, does not include the -s found in the English spelling, which is always a source of puzzlement to the French for whom the -s marks the plural. The GARONNE comes from

Spain, changes direction at Toulouse then flows west towards the Atlantic where Bordeaux lies on its estuary called the Gironde. Toulouse and Bordeaux are fine southern cities, ranking fourth and fifth in France.

As in many countries, a North/South divide exists. Northerners think people from the *midi* (the South) talk and boast a lot, that they make friends very easily but that this friendliness is somewhat superficial. They reckon the southerners have a different conception of time and never hurry. On the other hand, southerners pity northerners for living in what to them seems a cold climate which affects their character. *Les gens du Nord* are described as cold, hard-working, not very sociable and difficult to make friends with – but when friendship develops, it is a deep and long-lasting relationship.

In recent years efforts have been made to give the regions a greater say in the running of their own affairs, being reintroduced between 1972 and 1986 as larger administrative units to provide some sort of decentralization away from Paris and as a better framework for Europe. As they echo the old provinces, they are generally well accepted and the leader of the regional council is a powerful political figure.

Top Tip: To comply or not to comply. . .

Despite efforts at decentralization in recent years, the French administrative structure remains extremely centralized and hierarchical. Not surprisingly, therefore, it is a kind of national sport for the French to try to beat the system and avoid complying with decisions made in higher places. Behaviour which, in other countries, might be regarded as cheating, is looked on as perfectly acceptable. The attitude seems to be: Why should one obey silly regulations?

2

French Attitudes to Foreigners

[& Vice Versa!]

Getting the facts right . . .

THE FRANCE-ENGLAND RIVALRY

Old clichés die hard and France and England have had enough poisonous history between them to fill textbooks with one-sided arrogance: from the Hundred Years' War and Joan of Arc as enemy or saint, to Gare d'Austerlitz in Paris and Waterloo Station in London referring to Napoleon as a hero or a crushed dictator – depending on who you are.

A more recent example which might shed light on how the same event can be interpreted in painfully different ways is what the British have called 'the spirit of Dunkirk', a meaningless phrase in France. It should act as a warning to any visitors not to assume that their nation is gratefully remembered anywhere, even in allied countries.

The 1940 'miraculous' evacuation of over 300,000 troops by an amazing assortment of British boats from the Dunkirk area which at the time was surrounded by German forces, evokes solidarity in the face of adversity for the British, but a cynical betrayal for the French who saw the British evacuated first, while some 40,000 French soldiers were left to the Germans. Similarly, some French prisoners-of-war in Germany may have deep personal reasons to remember their captors more kindly than the Allied liberators.

Learned articles in French historical publications talk of anti-Americanism disappearing from French university circles whereas francophobia seems to be growing in American academe, and they retrace the various stages of delusion among each side concerning political, economic or intellectual interference or perception of interference. The de Gaulle era was particularly fertile, when the challenge for France was to obtain prosperity, consumer goods and technology with American help and yet retain its Frenchness.

By establishing a policy of independence from the USA, the resentment which used to be expressed graphically by graffiti of 'Yankees go home' daubed on walls bearing the standard *'Défense d'afficher'* ('notices prohibited'), evaporated. A reassessment of the so-called colonization of France has taken place and it is to be hoped that American academics guilty of francophobia will also come to realize that the projection of what may only be internal disputes onto the international scene is rarely productive. A good game, maybe?

HAUTE COUTURE

If one now switches to the realm of *haute couture*, one may be forgiven for being perplexed. The Home News page of a British daily recently carried lengthy reports on 'Paris fashion'; the odd connection between home and Paris possibly being explained by the fact that two British designers, A. McQueen and J. Galliano, newly-appointed heads of Givenchy and Dior couture houses respectively, were showing their first collections. Talent knows no borders indeed if they triumph in Paris. One also learns, however, that 'Britons' French couture staff 'cut up rough' (i.e. were extremely dissatisfied) and disrupted catwalk shows with fliers explaining that 'they [McQueen and Galliano] are very inexperienced and do not realize the time it takes to produce proper work'.

This report of worries amongst the *petites mains* (little hands, or expert seamstresses) was soon followed by metaphorical custard pies flying between the top nobs themselves, with Yves Saint-Laurent just about recovering from the vulgarity of the young English invaders whilst they kindly suggest retirement to the golden oldie so obviously 'out of fashion'!

Oh, dear! Despite dire predictions that the end is nigh for *haute couture*, 1997 may well prove to bring a revival in its fortunes, while the optimistic Anglo-Saxon press asserts that 'America and Italy may now be competing in the lucrative business of designer sportswear . . . – but only Paris has couture – the jewel in the crown – as well as a national heritage . . . .

Not many of us are going to be affected by the extinction or resurrection of Parisian *haute couture*, but it seems to function powerfully as a cultural icon linking something perceived as typically French and the rest of the world. Will it be saved by new foreign blood in the context of grinding globalization, with only 2,000 clients left worldwide compared with 200,000 in 1943?

The situation is suitably amusing and refers us to other convoluted attitudes which in turn divide French public opinion concerning its responses to foreign products and influences, ranging from Coca-cola, MacDonalds, Walt Disney films and theme parks to NATO and especially the English language. Several examples will be given in different chapters.

'ENTENTE CORDIALE'

The 'entente cordiale' is, however, fortunately a phrase common to both British and French language and culture and with us to stay. It did not come about easily, but King Edward VII, '*le roi charmeur*', conquered the anglophobia of the French with his personal touch at the turn of the twentieth century. Even popular songs begrudgingly admitted he was welcome in France since:

> *Quand il n'était que prince /*
> *De son sale pays [..] / Il venait à Paris [..] /*
> *Et ne quittait la table / Que huit jours après!*

('When he was but a Prince in his rotten country, he came to Paris and only left the table a week later.') As a return gesture, the French President was feted in London and treated to a chorus of British and French sailors on the stage, whilst a French and an English comedienne dressed respectively as Marianne and Britannia, joined hands to sing together the National anthem and *La Marseillaise*, a feat no military endeavour had ever achieved.

Supersonic Concord(e) – they still cannot agree on how to spell that magic name – is nowadays proclaiming the official *entente* to the high heavens. Meanwhile, in a more down-to-earth, *Le Shuttle* sort of way, continuing the tradition of promoting such *entente*, is *Tandem*, a Franco-British arts review, produced by the French Institute in London as a bilingual magazine with support from the British Council in Paris. It informs potential advertisers that 25,000 copies are published quarterly, an indication of the rich seam of Franco-British relations and that its 'readers are young, cultured, French or British, francophile or simply curious about what is happening across the Channel and like to go to France to live '*à la française*'.

THE OTHER FACES OF FRANCE

As a contrast to Paris, with all its historic images of romance, style and singular prowess, it is necessary to introduce an enduring aspect of French life which makes sense to foreign visitors because the French believe in it so strongly themselves: this is the countryside, or Deep France, ('*la France profonde*') which commands such an attachment.

But is there another face of France – one linked to racism? It is true to say that, sadly, this 'face' has emerged – confirmed in recent electoral gains by the National Front in four towns in southern France. Democratic demonstrations have, however, prevented the government from passing more laws pandering to feelings of insecurity manipulated by the extreme-right.

A February 1997 cover of *Le Nouvel Observateur*, a well-known French weekly, graphically shows how French society is struggling not to let its century-old reputation of being a fraternal land of freedom open to newcomers be sullied. It featured a 'Stop' roadsign with the legend 'NO TO RACIST FRANCE'. For whether the majority of the people realize it or not, the population of present-day France contains one-third of inhabitants who were foreigners one, two or three generations ago, making France the largest melting-pot in Europe.

So pick and choose your own feelings and attitudes to France. You are following in the path of many others who have enjoyed the idiomatic ways of the natives for a multitude of reasons. All of them have found it, if not always a cosy experience, at least a worthwhile challenge.

Top Tip: An old saying. . .

Remember the old saying that every civilized person has two countries: their own and France. Your genuine liking for or desire to like France will be warmly appreciated.

3

Meeting People

Winter sport

People shake hands when they meet and before parting again. It is usual for the senior person to proffer his or her hand first. If you enter a room where there are several people, shake hands with everyone; failing to shake hands might be interpreted as a sign of hostility, so it is important not to forget the handshake.

When you greet people, the proper way is to say: '*Bonjour monsieur*' to a man, '*Bonjour, madame*' to a woman, '*Bonjour, mademoiselle*' to a young lady.

French children are drilled to learn the polite formulae; always adding *madame, mademoi-*

selle, monsieur after **all** greetings (not just *Bonjour*, but *Au revoir* (Goodbye) and *Bonsoir* (Good evening); *Pardon* is very useful before asking for directions or the time. Keep '*Salut!*' (Hi!) to greet **back** a well-known person who first uses this familiar expression.

The French tend to be rather formal and do not use first names easily. They might be friends and still address each other with '*Monsieur X*' or '*Madame Y*'. Things are changing with the younger generation, but to be on the safe side, never use the first name unless you have been expressly asked to do so; otherwise, it might be resented as being too familiar.

French people have two ways of addressing each other: the formal *vous*; or the more familiar *tu*, which is reserved for their family and close friends – or even colleagues in certain circles.

Top Tip: How to address your mother-in-law

Even the French hesitate between *tu* and *vous*. How do you address your mother-in-law? It is for the most senior person to suggest a switch to *tu*. If your mother-in-law does not, then you are stuck with *vous* for the next half-century or so. Conversely, young or more junior people who are invited to use *tu* may find it quite difficult. People of the same age or similar background coming together for the first time may also be unsure of the right form to use. It will therefore be fun for you to listen to conversations and notice what is going on around you.

Instead of shaking hands, relatives and close friends kiss each other (two, three or four times depending on the region where you are staying).

Top Tip: Avoid familiarity in business

You might call a colleague of yours who is a friend by his first name and address him with *tu* when you are at home or alone, but you should revert to *monsieur* and *vous* when you are back at work and in official meetings. The French tend not to mix their private life with the world of work.

Once again, take heart: most French people have been left with one cheek in the air because they expected to receive a further kiss. Everyone is happy to laugh together! Kisses are also conveyed in correspondence: *Grosses bises, gros baisers, Je vous embrasse*, are all simply equivalent of the English *Love* (all equally shocking because out of place if taken literally!)

WRITING LETTERS

The reverse does, however, also happen in letters: the two coded British formulae *Yours sincerely* and *Yours faithfully* are woefully inadequate when compared with the time-honoured French formal endings which take such an effort to master and so long to write, but are a real feather in your cap once you have remembered them:

> *Veuillez agréer, Madame/Monsieur/ Mademoiselle, l'expression de mes sentiments dévoués/les meilleurs*

As you may guess, your choice should match the person addressed at the top of the letter as *Madame*, or other. You will **not** have included *Cher* or *Chère* in front of *Monsieur* or *Madame* as this would be judged too familiar. The French may live in a republic but some forms of polite social etiquette do smack of courtly protocol.

CONVERSATIONAL TECHNIQUES

Compared to Northern Europeans, French people are extrovert; their conversation is often reinforced by gestures. When taking part in a discussion in a group, they do not wait until someone has finished making a point, they interrupt and put forward their own ideas. This is not considered impolite; quick exchanges are the rule. If the discussion gets heated, the person who speaks or shouts loudest seems to win the argument. To an outsider this might appear aggressive, but not in the eyes of the French, who are brought up to be competitive.

Conversation is frequently peppered with witty remarks. The French have a satirical sense of humour – but at other people's expense. If someone makes fun of them, they are touchy or even hurt; they consider it rude and defend themselves in an unexpectedly forceful manner.

HOME & FAMILY LIFE

It is said that foreigners, although they find French people friendly enough, are disappointed because they are not readily invited into French homes. The reason is that the French only want the best for their guests; everything has to be perfect, especially the food. Lunch or dinner offered to guests will invariably require considerable preparation which is one reason why a formal invitation may not happen straight away. But when it comes, it is a very special treat indeed. Be prepared to spend several hours at the dining table; for the French, a meal is the ideal social occasion, involving plenty of eating, drinking and talking.

French people are individualistic, insisting on doing things their own way even if it means bending the rules; but at the same time they seldom rebel against the constraints of family life. When they do, it is fairly traumatic. Many a novel refers to the tensions involved.

Youngsters tend to stay at home much longer than their Northern European counterparts. Even when they start working, it is not unusual for them to stay with their parents until they marry. If they enter higher education, they attend the university nearest to their home. Children remain close to their grandparents, uncles, aunts and cousins.

Sunday lunch, therefore, is invariably a family affair often including relatives living in the same district. This is especially the case in the provinces where families are not as scattered.

French people are generally reluctant to move from one region to another even if job prospects are better; the only exception is moving from the provinces to Paris. The aim of most people's career seems to be to become senior enough to be able to choose being posted **back** to their native regions.

THE STATE & RELIGION

Traditionally France is a Catholic country but in recent times the church has lost a great deal of its influence. Although many people might not be church-goers, they still celebrate religious festivals which punctuate the different stages of life: birth, adolescence and marriage. *Baptême* for babies, *communion solonnelle* for 12-year-olds and weddings are occasions for big family gatherings with huge meals lasting several hours.

The French seem to have devised ways of putting Religion and State on a par so that everyone is happy. This is shown in their main festivals, at winter and summer-time. Christmas and New Year

'Vive la France'

are celebrated very much in the same way, with similar meals at odd times called by the same name (*réveillon*). The storming of the old prison of the Bastille in Paris is the event celebrated as the Republic's founding date on 14 July, with days off, dancing and fireworks. One month later, on 15 August, the same type of celebrations occur but this time for the Assumption, which few people realize is the Roman Catholic festival of the raising to heaven of the Virgin Mary.

With the arrival of many North African immigrants, Islam has become the second most important religion in France. There is also a Protestant minority which plays a fairly important role, despite being small in number; many of its members occupy leading positions in politics or the civil service. The population also includes a Jewish community.

LANGUAGES & TRAVEL

In France, the older generation are not very good at speaking other languages. Foreign language teaching used to be very formal, based on learning grammar and the study of literary texts and not aimed at communicating effectively with foreigners. French was the language spoken by diplomats and educated foreigners visiting France. French people were not really keen on travelling and living abroad except perhaps in the French colonies; they were so confident in the superiority of everything French that they did not feel any need to communicate in another language.

Now attitudes and teaching methods have changed a great deal. Foreign language learning is encouraged at an early age, even at kindergarten and primary school. Youngsters are keen on acquiring foreign languages, mostly English, German, Spanish and to a lesser extent Italian and Russian. In many business schools English is compulsory and work experience abroad is highly valued.

Top Tip: The French may reply in English!

Do not be upset if your attempts at communicating in French are thwarted by people talking back to you in English. It is mostly the case that they want to practise their skills and also make you feel at ease. Do not bear the French people a grudge, therefore, for not being able to use your French even in France! You will have plenty of other opportunities when French is the only means of communication and people will greatly appreciate the efforts you made to learn their language.

The best preparation for conversational French is to use cassettes as well as phrase-books because pronunciation is based on vowel sounds and not on consonants which are very often unvoiced at the end of words unless they precede a word starting with a vowel, producing the famous *liaison*, e.g., 'comment allez-vous?' There are no stressed syllables. All this means that words like 'telephone' or 'table' which are written in the same way in French and English do sound quite different. Despite your misgivings, French pronunciation is easier to master than English because there are definite rules of articulation and combination. Another good game in prospect!

4

French Homes

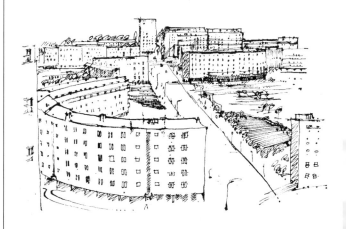

Modern apartment blocks near Paris'

Rented apartments rather than private houses are the norm in French towns and cities. The entrance to each apartment block used to be watched by the *concierge* or *gardien* who was in charge of distributing the mail and keeping the staircases clean, but in modern buildings you have to press the intercommunication button of the person you want to visit, state your name and he or she will open the main entrance by remote control. Individual doors are fitted with a brass plaque or a card carrying the name of the occupant.

If you do not see any such communication devices, you may be stuck a long time outside the *porte cochère*, or former carriage entrance, especially with old buildings in Paris. So here is the *'sesame'* formula: Is there a button to press? Then do so but although there will be a buzzing noise, do not expect any answer; it is the signal for you to push the door open. During the day, it will probably be enough to get in. Once inside the communal corridor, you may find a grill barring your (and the tramps') way. At this stage, you will have access to the interphone and the letter boxes.

At night or for all sorts of reasons, you may find that pressing the button and leaning on the door will serve no purpose: you can only enter if you have been given the secret code to tap on the pad next to the button. If you have been invited and cannot get in, the only solution is to telephone from the nearest booth or café. The first time can be extremely frustrating; then you learn to ask for the code and to jot it down for the next visit.

The dream of every Frenchman is to have his own house built to his own specifications. On new housing estates you will find a great variety of houses surrounded by a clearly delimited garden. However, in order not to spoil the character of an area, regulations put a curb on the individuality and creativity of French builders. Houses have to be in keeping with the traditional buildings of the region. For example, in Brittany where roofs are

'The dream of every Frenchman . . .'

covered with slates, it is prohibited to use tiles which are traditionally used in the South.

Many town-dwellers have a second home. Because of the exodus from rural areas, increasing numbers of village houses and farm buildings are deserted and bought as *résidences secondaires* where city-dwellers spend their week-

Top Tip: Keep out of the kitchen!

If you are invited into a French home, remember that the kitchen may be a no-go area. Do not insist on helping to carry things from the table or doing the washing-up; you would only embarrass your host or hostess who would probably think you were being nosy. They want you to enjoy a beautiful meal and the company but not to be aware of, or take part in, the hard work which goes on behind the scenes.

ends and holidays. You do not have to be very rich to afford these properties, except in the most sought-after areas in the South, on the Riviera for instance, where prices are high.

5

Eating & Drinking

Le petit déjeuner – breakfast

Two cooked meals a day – lunch and an evening meal – are usually eaten in France. For breakfast, coffee is drunk (often with milk) out of a bowl rather than a cup; children drink either white coffee or chocolate. White crispy bread is spread with butter and jam. Figure-conscious people eat *biscotte*, a kind of toasted bread. On Sundays, the first one up buys freshly baked *croissants*.

Lunch-time usually lasts for two hours and whenever possible the whole family comes together. As schoolchildren start work at 8.30 am and finish at 4.30 pm or later, schools provide a canteen to cater for those who cannot go home.

Lunch usually consists of a main course which might be meat or fish and vegetables, preceded by a starter and followed by lettuce, cheese and/or a dessert. There is always a basket of bread on the table as French people eat bread

'People linger at table'

Top Tip: Don't wipe the plate clean!

Always break the bread with your fingers, never cut it. There are no side plates for bread, so do not worry if crumbs go all over the table. It is often assumed that the French use bread to clean their plates. Although they might occasionally indulge in this practice privately at home in order to eat a particularly delicious sauce, doing it in the presence of guests is considered bad manners.

throughout the meal, **except** with soup. However tempting fresh, crispy bread might be, refrain from nibbling at a piece before the meal actually starts or between courses, or your host will think you are desperately hungry.

As usual, the golden rule is to watch the natives, and do the same. The one rule of politeness you should try consciously to observe concerns the position of your hands when you eat. Because the rule, just like driving on the right on the other side of the Channel, is the exact opposite of the English one, it may produce unease at first. The sacred rule is to keep your left hand and wrist (not the elbow!) **on** the table during the meal, **not under**.

When children return from school, they have a *goûter* which consists of a piece of bread with a bar of chocolate or a pastry and a bowl of *café au lait* or *chocolat au lait*.

Most people finish work at 6.00 pm, consequently the evening meal does not start until 7.00 or 8.00 pm. The whole family gathers around the dining-table, even young children, and might well listen to or watch the news broadcast.

On Sundays, more members of the extended family may be reunited and meals are more elaborate. They are preceded by an *apéritif*, a drink like Martini or other fortified wines including *porto* (port), whisky, which is cheaper in France, and various brand names are discussed by enthusiastic connoisseurs, a typically French *pastis* (a drink flavoured with aniseed) or *Suze* (a bitter drink made with herbs).

Starters consist of salads, *charcuterie* (cold sliced meat and sausages) or shellfish. A special meal might have two main courses. Vegetables are sometimes served on their own after the main course. Refrain from using the salt and pepper cellars even if they are on the table; adding more spices would imply that the person who prepared the meal did not get it right. To refresh the palate lettuce tossed in oil and vinegar is served, followed by cheese. The meal ends with the dessert: cake or ice-cream for example, and fruit.

The *boulangerie* – bread for all tastes

People linger at the table, drink coffee and *digestifs* such as Cognac, Calvados (apple brandy) or *liqueurs*: Cointreau or Grand Marnier (orange-based), Chartreuse or Bénédictine (made with herbs). If you are a smoker, this is when you might light a cigarette. It would be very rude to smoke during the meal as it prevents you and others from properly tasting and appreciating the food the hostess has spent hours preparing.

WINE

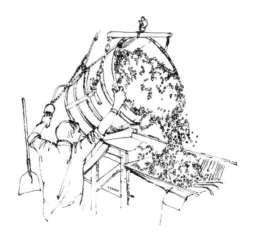

Wine-making: grapes into the press

Wine is the traditional drink. If it is ordinary table wine, it might be diluted with water to quench the thirst but if it is good quality wine, it is drunk straight in little sips. As soon as your glass is empty, it will be replenished; if you do not want to drink a lot, always leave something in your glass.

Top Tip: The secret of choosing wine

Drinking and enjoying wine is an art. For the experience to be perfect, wine has to have the right colour, smell and taste, and be at the right temperature. It is chosen to match the taste of the food of the different courses. This is why you should not bring a bottle of wine if you are invited because you will not know the menu. Champagne, however, is a possibility as is a quality spirit.

Different wines are served during the meal: *rosé* or *blanc sec* (dry white) with starters, *rouge* (red) with meat, dry white with fish, *blanc doux* (sweet white) with the dessert. Before drinking wipe your lips with your napkin and hold your glass by the stem in order not to leave marks on the glass which would prevent you from fully appreciating the colour and quality of the wine. The French can be lyrical about wine; they have very many words to describe the colour, smell and taste.

Although tap water is all right, French people insist on drinking bottled water. In a restaurant if you want to avoid the expense of mineral water (which can be very pricey) ask for *une carafe d'eau*, tap water which is provided free.

REGIONAL CUISINE & SPECIAL DISHES

The pattern of a French meal always remains the same, but the content can vary tremendously depending on the area. Due to its varied geography and climate, France has a great range of products which are used in rich and original regional cuisines. Normandy is famous for its specialities cooked in cream and apple brandy,

Brittany for its seafood, Burgundy for dishes cooked in wine, Périgord for poultry preserved in its own fat (*confit de canard or d'oie*) and dishes flavoured with truffles. If you are treated to '*foie gras*', do not insult your hosts by thinking it is mere *pâté*. Provence will offer dishes including olive oil, garlic, tomatoes and peppers. Northern areas use butter and onions, southern areas oil and garlic in their cooking. Although wine is drunk everywhere in France, cider is the traditional drink in the West and beer in the East and extreme North.

Important events of a private nature are celebrated with a special meal. Christmas and New Year, of course, are also occasions for a big meal: *le réveillon*. Traditionally, oysters, which are at their best at this time of the year, are served as starters, followed by a special choice of *charcuterie* which might well include *foie gras* (goose or duck liver preserved in its own fat). The main course is goose, capon or turkey served with chestnuts, followed by lettuce, a choice of cheeses and a cake shaped like a log. The *réveillon* takes place on Christmas Eve, and gifts are also exchanged between members of the family.

New Year's Eve is a similar occasion often celebrated with friends rather than relatives. It is called *la Saint-Sylvestre* because of the name of the saint remembered on that day in yesteryears. Greetings are exchanged at midnight and Champagne is drunk to toast the New Year. If you are in Paris, take your bottle and join the crowds milling on the Champs-Elysées, as traffic is banned for the night: it is a wonderful sight with all the Christmas decorations and floodlit monuments; but here is a word of caution concerning making your way back. Either be sure that you **do** know the time of the last metro train or be ready to foot it as taxis will have been booked long in advance.

French people are immensely proud of their cooking and wine; they are convinced that nothing is better. Even if your grasp of French is limited, be sure you show your appreciation of a meal by your facial expression – or by taking second helpings! Then you will be regarded as good company and worth inviting again. How about learning: *'Madame, votre cuisine est magnifique!'*

Be ready to taste new food; declining to sample a dish prepared by your host would be very rude. If you can speak some French, do not hesitate to ask questions about the food being served; besides consuming food, talking about it is a favourite French pastime. In so doing, your reputation will be greatly enhanced and you will

---

Top Tip: Be a good guest!

If you are invited for a meal, arrive promptly; the different stages will have been carefully timed, so do not put all the efforts of the cook at risk by arriving late. It is customary to present flowers to the hostess, but not chrysanthemums which in France are associated with death (they are put on graves on 1 November). Choose an odd number of flowers but avoid 13. A box of chocolates is also a traditional gift. **Remember that a bottle of wine is not a good idea.**

be respected as a foreigner who understands what really matters.

A meal is not just about food – conversation is almost as important. In a festive meal which can last several hours, there is plenty of time for discussion between courses. Although no topic is really taboo, talking about money is not welcome; asking a person how much he/she earns or what has been paid for a certain item would cause embarrassment.

THE RIGHT TOPICS FOR CONVERSATION

It goes without saying, of course, that certain topics are best avoided unless you are in a position to understand the language well, feel that you are on sympathetic wave-lengths and have some historical knowledge of events you may genuinely be interested to hear about from witnesses of the period; the Second World War is still a difficult subject for some and much more so the Algerian War and the sequels of decoloniza-tion and racism. You may, however, remember that most topics are touched upon with seemingly vindictive ardour at the end of the meal, *entre la poire et le fromage*, (between pear and cheese – a strange expression since fruit is always served after cheese) and yet with no hard feelings. It may just be a way of prolonging the twin pleasures of food and conversation.

Meals are treated seriously, even when matters of life and death are at stake. Fascinating details, for example, are known concerning Louis

XVI's last meals before he ascended the scaffold in 1793: according to Franklin, he had three soups, four entrées, three roast dishes, four sweet courses, fancy cakes, three compotes, three fruit dishes, Champagne, Bordeaux, Malvoisie, and Madeira wines followed by coffee!

In January 1996, President Mitterand died of cancer. From the many biographies published, one learns of his last painful days; for the *réveillon* of *la Saint-Sylvestre* at his country house, although unable to sit at the table, he insisted on the traditional fare with his family and close friends and ate even more than them, downing three dozen oysters, two ortolans as well as *foie gras* and capon. Then he went back to Paris alone with his doctor; there he refused to touch food again and died a few days later.

WHERE TO EAT AND DRINK

A great range of restaurants can be found throughout France. You do not have to spend a lot of money to obtain a good meal. To a certain extent, the prices can reflect the quality of service rather than that of the food provided. For example, in the lower price range, the cutlery probably will not be changed with every course. The menu and prices are displayed outside restaurants. Occasionally, in exclusive restaurants ladies are handed menus without prices, a custom left over from the times when women were always entertained and not supposed to know at what cost.

Top Tip: How to order steak

It is worth trying smaller places specializing in regional cooking but if you are in a hurry, do as the French do and order a *steak frites* (steak and chips). When ordering steak, keep in mind that to a French cook *saignant* (rare) means the steak is just sealed on both sides. If you like your meat pink ask for *à point* or *bien cuit* if you cannot face under-cooked meat.

Often it is better value to choose a *menu* (set menu) rather than *à la carte*. A set menu might include wine, whereas a very reasonably-priced meal can become much more expensive when you order wine separately as restaurateurs make most of their profits on drinks. If you are not sure which wine would be appropriate for a particular dish, ask for advice - the restaurateur will take pride in choosing the right wine for you. If you decided to order something completely unsuitable, such as red wine with fish, for example, he probably would not be able to resist putting you right straight away.

If you are travelling and want to stop for a meal on the main road, *Routiers* restaurants are to be recommended. They cater mainly (but not exclusively) for long-distance drivers, providing good and very substantial meals at a reasonable price; the longer the queue of articulated lorries in the car park, the better the food is likely to be.

*B*rasseries also provide meals but the choice of dishes is not as great as in restaurants. You are expected to order a full meal in a restaurant but in a brasserie ordering just the main course is fine.

A Routiers restaurant

*C*rêperies are places which specialize in pancakes, sweet 'crêpes' and savoury 'galettes'. In Brittany and Normandy, the pancakes are accompanied by delicious sparkling cider served in bowls.

*C*afés are convivial places where friends meet, chat and watch the world go by. They are open from early morning until late at night, serving not only coffee but also alcoholic and soft drinks; one favourite is *citron pressé*, freshly squeezed lemon juice with water, ice-cubes and sugar to taste served in a large glass.

Cafés also prepare snacks: sandwiches with *jambon* (ham), *saucisson* (cold sausage), *rillette* (pork spread), *fromage* (cheese) or a hot *croque monsieur*, a ham and cheese toasted sandwich.

Cafés-Tabac, which display a red carrot-shaped sign outside, not only sell tobacco but also stamps, phonecards and, in Paris, Metro/bus tickets.

6

Business Contacts

La Defense, Paris – centre for trade, business and industry

French business people, especially the older generation, behave very formally. You are expected to dress smartly, shake hands with everybody, address individuals with the formal *vous* and use titles correctly. More and more young people speak English. Women are increasingly represented at management level in certain industries, particularly in Paris.

In French companies the managing director (*PDG* – *Président Directeur Général*) exercises control to an extent that some foreigners may find surprising. His authority is based on competence; he takes all the important decisions himself and his attitude to his subordinates is aloof.

If you wish to contact senior executives, do not rely too much on their 'secretary', who does not usually have the authority to make appointments.

Sometimes, it may be difficult to organize meetings because French executives tend not to commit themselves until the last moment. Punctuality is expected of you, but you might have to wait if another engagement is considered more important than yours. Business appointments can be made during office hours, usually from 9.00 am to 6.00 pm. Some business people do not like to start the day in a hurry and will not see people before 9.30 am or even later, although you may be given a late appointment after 6.00 pm. In the world of show business do not expect anything to happen before 11.30 am.

When drawing up contracts, the French side will insist on precision; a verbal agreement is only a preliminary to a written agreement, which alone is legally binding. As long as written documents have not been signed, you cannot be sure of having secured anything.

Most people take their holidays in August, and this month is therefore best avoided as far as promoting business is concerned.

Top Tip: Pay the bill & be precise!

Business is still often done over an elaborate meal or perhaps during coffee at the end of it. The person who is trying to secure a contract pays for the meal. During negotiations you are expected to be clear, consistent and precise; things have to be logical to be accepted. French people appreciate abstract discussion and projects which are well thought out but do not care much about pragmatism.

The French style of letter-writing is extremely formal. Do not be surprised if after a friendly meeting you receive a letter written in convoluted language. The French are notorious for taking a long time in answering letters – if you do need a prompt answer send a fax or telephone.

7

Travelling Around

TGV – *Train à Grande Vitesse*

If you drive in France, remember the following speed limits:

130 kph (80 mph) on **motorways**
90 kph (55 mph) on **other roads**
50 kph (30 mph) in **built-up areas**

Not all French drivers observe these limits, but if they are caught speeding, there are on-the-spot fines. A solidarity has developed among drivers and if you see a vehicle coming in the opposite direction flashing its headlights, it is a warning that *gendarmes* (policemen) are not far away, and for a few miles motorists will adjust their speed and behave as exemplary drivers.

Furthermore, French drivers tend not to be too considerate towards pedestrians – even at pedestrian crossings. In order to remedy this, speed ramps are being introduced. They are made so high that it would ruin the suspension of your car if you were to drive over them at more than 20 kph. At last pedestrians in France have a chance to cross the roads with some degree of safety!

As a rule, you have to give way to traffic coming from the right, even if you are on a main road. Roundabouts are becoming more numerous but there seem to be no uniform rules as to who has right of way. When you arrive at a roundabout, a sign will advise you if you can proceed or not; *Cédez le passage* or *Vous n'avez pas la priorité* indicates you have to give way to traffic already on the roundabout.

Except for short sections around towns, French motorways are *autoroutes à péage*, toll motorways. You pay at the entrance by throwing coins into a kind of basket or pushing them into a slot, or you are given a ticket and pay at the exit. It is also possible to use credit cards. The motorway network is relatively new in France and very often large sections run parallel to the *routes nationales* (main roads) which are very good and signposted with N followed by a number; D roads are *routes départementales* which are narrower.

Driving in Paris can be very frustrating because of the one-way system and the lack of parking spaces. Parisians have developed an amazing skill at parking in the smallest gap, great use being made of bumpers to enlarge the space between two parked cars. In the centre, most parking spaces are *payant*, with a high hourly rate in an attempt to encourage commuters to use public transport rather than their own cars. August is the only time when driving in Paris is easy – because so many Parisians are away on holiday.

Driving on main roads is best avoided on public holidays during the summer. As most people take their holidays in July or August, on the first and last weekend of these months traffic is at its worst, with long tailbacks near large cities. Statistics for road accidents also warn of danger around the times of the two summer festivals mentioned earlier,

Top Tip: Driving on the Périphérique

If you want to avoid driving through Paris, use the *Boulevard Périphérique* (the ring road). However, at peak hours it can be heavily congested, so make sure you stay in the right-hand lane (the slow lane) in order not to miss your exit. Remember which one you need. If you miss it, use the next one! Many sections of the *Périphérique* were built on what were once the fortifications of Paris, and most exits are called *Porte de. . .* which means 'gate'.

14 July and 15 August since people exchange visits and attend late-night events in a celebratory mood!

In an attempt to reduce drinking and driving, police apply the law rigorously, and driving licences can be withdrawn on the spot.

The wearing of seatbelts is compulsory and it is illegal to have a child in the front seat either strapped in or on the passenger's lap.

RAILWAYS

Trains are reliable, fast and clean but they tend to be crowded at weekends and during public holidays. On these occasions it is advisable to book your seat in advance.

PUBLIC HOLIDAYS

New Year
Easter and **Easter Monday**
1 May, **Labour Day**
8 May, **End of World War II**
Ascension day in May
Pentecôte (Whitsun) at the end of May
14 July, **National Day**
15 August, **Assumption Day**
1 November, **All Saints' Day**
11 November, **Remembrance Day**
25 December, **Christmas Day**

It is compulsory to book your seat in advance on the TGV (*Train à Grande Vitesse* – high-speed train).

The SNCF (French Railways) makes great efforts to please customers, besides making sure that trains run on time. Trains are clean and the seats are pleasant and comfortable. In *trains corail* (express trains) there is a special carriage where children can play, and during the summer, entertainment is provided on the main lines at no extra cost. A carriage can house an exhibition, a cinema, become a stage for artists or offer you specialities of the region you are travelling through.

Before boarding a train you must validate your ticket by pushing it into a small machine which punches a hole and stamps the date. (The magic word for this process is *'composter'*.) There are frequent ticket inspections on trains and inspectors speak foreign languages, so you cannot easily get away with pretending you do not understand. A hefty fine is levied on the spot from *all* offenders!

In France coaches are not an alternative to trains, they only go where trains do not go.

'Marianne' (see p. 70)

Top Tip: Using the Metro

The *Metro* (underground/subway) is the cheapest and fastest way to travel in Paris. Each line takes its name from the last stop, which means that on a return journey the same line will have a different name. If you have to change, follow the sign *Correspondance* and the appropriate name of the line.

It is cheaper to buy a booklet of 10 tickets, so ask for a *carnet*. These tickets can also be used on buses. They can be bought not only at Metro stations but also at newsagents and Cafés-Tabac. On the Metro you only need one ticket whatever the length of your journey and irrespective of the number of times you change lines.

USING PUBLIC TRANSPORT IN PARIS

On buses you need 1 or 2 tickets according to the length of your journey and you have to pay again whenever you board a new bus. Some bus lines can be a cheap alternative to sightseeing tours as they take you past the main sights. This is true of line 72 between the Hôtel de Ville (Town Hall) and the Eiffel Tower, for example.

Keep your ticket until you leave the bus or Metro as you might be required to produce it for inspection.

Try avoiding the rush hours (between 7.00 and 9.00 in the morning, then 6.00 and 7.30 in the evening) when it would be difficult to extricate yourself and your luggage from the carriage and you would be unpopular with fellow passengers.

Luggage is not accepted on buses at any time. Queuing is virtually unknown at bus stops, so it is necessary to assert yourself — sometimes with vigorous use of the elbows.

8

Out & About

local open-air market

As in other parts of Europe, large shopping centres and supermarkets are replacing small shops, but French people still rely on corner shops and markets for certain kinds of food. The French like their bread fresh and crisp, and in towns they are prepared to go twice a day to the baker's shop which opens at 7.30 am and remains open until 7.00 or 8.00 pm; it even opens until noon on Sundays. Other shops open later, at 8.00 or 9.00 am, but all of them are shut for two or three hours at midday.

POST OFFICES

Hours of business are usually between 8.00 am and 7.00 pm on weekdays and until 12 noon on Saturdays. Stamps can also be obtained from Bars-Tabac. Letter-boxes are yellow.

The public phone system in France is comprehensive and includes even the smallest villages. Coin-operated phones are fast disappearing, and in large towns most public phones require a *télécarte* (phonecard). If you intend spending some time in France it might be worth buying a *télécarte* with 50 or 100 *unités*. You can buy *télécartes* at post offices, railway stations, Bars-Tabac (with the red carrot sign) and some newsagents.

Fish shop in the heart of Paris

As from 1997, the telephone network has been upgraded and made easier, putting every call on a ten-digit number, whether you are making a local or regional call. If you wish to telephone abroad, you now only have to dial 00 + the code for the country. All this is clearly shown inside the street telephone kiosks, with the names of countries, and a map of France showing that Paris and region (*Ile de France*) now add 01 in front of your correspondent's number, 02 for the North-West, 03 for the North-East, 04 for the South-East and 05 for the South-West.

Check whether you have been given a 10-digit number, in which case you do not need to add anything; if not, a recorded voice will tell you to add one of the above, which will, after all, only test your listening skills up to 5. If you are given a *Numéro vert* to call, it will start with 008 and it will be free. Most mobile numbers will now show as 06 and there are a few more specialized services with other prefixes.

If you go to a post-office, you are entitled to consult the *Minitel* free because it replaced book-form directories years ago. It is a type of Internet system. After giving the screen and keyboard free to every household, a huge profit was made on the calls especially to *les lignes roses* for adult services. You can use your Minitel to book seats on trains, planes and in theatres as well as organize your bank services. Some say its very success is hindering the uptake of Internet provisions.

BANKS & MUSEUMS

Most banks open between 9.00 am and 12 noon, and from 2.00 pm till 4.00 pm on weekdays; also from 9.30 am to 12 noon on Saturdays. In certain areas they are closed all day on Saturday or Monday. They are closed on Sundays and public holidays. Be aware of the security airlock between the two entrance doors. Press the red button, and when it shows green the door will be unlocked. Repeat for the second door.

Museums and monuments are usually closed all day on Tuesdays. This applies to the main category of 'national' museums. The 'local' ones tend to be closed on Mondays, allowing you, therefore, to plan visits on both days. By far the best way to see what is on as soon as you arrive in Paris is to buy either *Pariscope* or *l'Officiel des spectacles* for about two francs and study it seriously. The prices of the shows are indicated with a bewildering array of reductions for students, pensioners or large families at different times on different days. A list of abbreviations is thankfully to be found before the rubric.

PETROL STATIONS

Sometimes attendants are reluctant to accept cheques or even refuse them for amounts over 100 francs; but credit cards are acceptable.

WHERE TO STAY

The *Office du Tourisme* or *Syndicat d'initiative* (Tourist Information Office) will help you in choosing from a range of hotels rated from one to four stars.

Usually you pay for the room rather than per person, and breakfast is not included. Some hotels which also run restaurants expect you to have a meal there if you want a room, although such a requirement is not legal.

If you wish to stay in a Bed and Breakfast establishment look for the sign *Chambre d'hôtes*. In the countryside *Table d'hôtes* might be on offer as well; this means you can have a meal and take the opportunity to sample local specialities at a reasonable price.

If you plan a longer stay in an area, *gîtes* are an interesting option. These are self-catering holiday homes, very often old farmhouses or houses of character which have been renovated.

Youth Hostels, *Auberges de Jeunesse*, are not generally as numerous as in certain other European countries.

PUBLIC CONVENIENCES

Some public toilets have attendants who will not let you go in unless you put the required amount of money in a little dish. French people are surprised by the reluctance of some foreigners to use *toilettes turques*; they cannot see what all the fuss is about. Instead of having a toilet seat, you stand on slightly raised foot-rests and squat. Just make sure you unlock the door and are ready to exit swiftly before you flush the toilet.

Top Tip: Using a public toilet – in Paris

The famous free-standing urinals of Paris are now museum pieces and have been replaced by unobtrusive unisex cabins. Green and red lights have replaced the *libre* or *occupé* signs. The door opens when you push coins into a slot. Never go two at a time to save 2F: the automatic cleaning of the whole cublicle starts when the door closes after your exit.

If no public toilets are available, you can go into a café; they will not mind your using their facilities if you leave a tip.

9

Useful Words & Phrases

WORDS YOU ALREADY KNOW

hôtel, restaurant, banque, taxi, poste, téléphone, toilette, bus.

SIGNS

entrée	entrance
déviation	diversion
sortie	exit
péage	toll
interdit	prohibited
douane	Customs
défense de . . .	prohibited
gare	railway station
non fumeur	non-smoking

hommes	gentlemen
femmes	ladies
cédez le passage	give way
vous n'avez pas la priorité	give way
priorité piétons	pedestrians have right of way

WHAT YOU CAN SAY

oui	yes
non	no
pardon	excuse me
bonjour	good morning/day
bonsoir	good evening
au revoir	goodbye
s'il vous plait	please
parlez-vous anglais?	do you speak English?
comment?	I beg your pardon
je ne comprends pas	I don't understand
où est. . .?	where is. . .?
quand?	when?
c'est combien?	how much is it?
une chambre	a room
avec douche	with shower
avec salle de bain	with bathroom

WHAT YOU MIGHT HEAR

Bon séjour	Have a nice stay
Bon voyage	Have a good journey
Bonne année	Happy New Year
Joyeux Noël	Merry Christmas

Facts About France

The capital of France is Paris with a population of 2,152,423. Other major cities include the country's most important port, Marseilles (1,230,936), Lyons (1,262,223) a major trade centre and home of the oldest stock exchange in France dating from 1506, and Lille (959,234).

The west of France borders the Atlantic Ocean (see map p. 12) and produces moist temperate conditions, while the east of the country has the cold winters and hot summers that are typical of central Europe. The northern parts of France are bordered by the English Channel or La Manche (depending on which side you live) and share a climate similar to that of southern Britain, while the south has the hot summers of the Mediterranean countries, together with the risk of drought conditions and forest fires. The average temperatures in Paris range from 1-6C in January to 16-19C in July.

Mont Blanc, in the French Alps, is the highest peak in Europe at 4807 metres (15,771 feet).

French Currency

The French currency is the Franc which is equal to 100 centimes. The denominations in notes are 500F, 200F, 100F, 50F and 20F and in coins are 20F, 10F, 5F, 2F, 1F, 50 centimes, 20 centimes, 10 centimes and 5 centimes. Credit cards are widely accepted in France and Travellers' cheques easily cashed.

The Eiffel Tower, which dominates the Parisian skyline, was built in 1887-9 and is 300m (984ft) high.

French is spoken by 58 million people in France, and is a first language in Belgium and Switzerland. It is also used outside Europe: in the Quebec province of Canada, in North Africa and many countries of West Africa, in Madagascar and Mauritius, the West Indies (Martinique, Guadeloupe and

Haiti), South America (French Guiana) and South East Asia (Vietnam and Cambodia). The commonwealth of French speakers is called '*La Francophonie*'.

Liberté, Égalité, Fraternité is the motto of the French Republic, which you will see written on public buildings and coins.

Marianne

Marianne is the symbol of the French Republic, a female figure found on stamps and coins. Every town hall has a bust of her, sometimes modelled on a famous French woman, from Brigitte Bardot in the sixties to a Chanel model in the eighties.

Education is compulsory in France between the ages of six and 16.

Most families send their children to state schools (*Écoles publiques*) which are free and considered to provide the best education. The majority go to nursery schools before they reach the compulsory school age of six. Wednesday is a free day for school children but many have lessons on Saturday morning. The French education system is very competitive; children have to repeat a class if they have not achieved a certain level by the end of the school year. The National Curriculum issued by the Ministry of Education prescribes in detail what has to be learned.

Since the beginning of the twentieth century church and state have been strictly separated and religion is not taught in state schools.

There is no state religion in France, but the vast majority of the population, approximately 81.4%, are of Roman Catholic origin, with 6.9% being Muslims and 1.7% being Protestants. (For more details of these religions please see the companion series *The Simple Guides to World Religions*.)

Private schools (*écoles privées*) are mainly Roman Catholic and have their own ethos. The curriculum, however, is the same as in state schools as they are under contract to the government which pays the teachers' salaries and contributes to the upkeep of the buildings. Fees are therefore very low and parents tend to choose their children's' schools according to local convenience, reputation and facilities rather than religious feelings.

The French take great pride in their long and prestigious literary tradition. However, in schools, literature is not considered as important as mathematics, an ability which is generally used as a gauge of intelligence, perhaps because it demands skills in logical thinking.

In higher education, universities are open to anyone who has passed the *Baccalauréat* (secondary education leaving certificate) but there is also a system of highly selective *Grandes Écoles* where many future top executives, civil servants and politicians are educated.

Every young man over 18 used to have to do military service, although the length of time was being reduced more and more and civil community service could be done instead. Since 1997, boys born after 1979 are called up in front of a commission called *rendez-vous du citoyen*; it will be the same for girls after 2002. The new system enables young people to choose whether to serve in the military or in civic, humanitarian projects for ten months of compulsory SMA (adapted military service).

Boules

In summer, the French like playing *boules*. The aim is to roll solid steel balls as close as possible to a little wooden ball, the *cochonnet* (= 'piggy'). You can throw them to try and dislodge an opponent's ball. Any patch of ground will do, from a village square to a garden path.

Cycling is very popular. The famous Tour de France race is followed by millions during July. The final stage ends on the Champs Elysées in Paris and the winner wears a yellow vest, the coveted *maillot jaune*.

In winter, an increasing number of people go to ski resorts in the Alps or the Pyrénées. Since the law entitles employees to five weeks paid holiday each year, people tend to take three or four weeks in summer, keeping a week or two for a winter break.

France has a long and varied coastline which attracts many holiday-makers who are keen on water sports. But you do not have to be at the seaside to go sailing, water-skiing or windsurfing. Local authorities have made great efforts to develop the potential offered by lakes and have created numerous artificial ones.

In order to attract the tourist industry, regional authorities have renovated waterways which had fallen into neglect when rail and road traffic became more profitable. Hiring a barge or a small boat is now an available option for people who wish to explore a region in an unusual and relaxing way! The *'Canal du Midi'* is especially popular.

Ministry for Culture

French people are immensely proud of their cultural heritage; they even have a Ministry for Culture. In summer many theatre and music festivals are organized in the provinces. Ancient monuments are used as the setting for plays and concerts even in remote areas. Floodlit castles are the venue for *Son et Lumière* – elaborate performances during which local actors recreate historical events.

The French take cinema very seriously and call it the 'seventh art'. French film-makers concentrate on analysing human relationships within the family or a small group of people rather than aiming for spectacular productions. It is true to say that the French have a 'love/hate' response to Disney.

Jazz music is an important genre in France. In recent years, popular music has been enriched by musical traditions from Africa, in the same way as plastic arts were greatly influenced by African art in the twenties. A strong tradition of *chansons* is still thriving, in which songs are similar to poems and the words matter more than the accompanying music.

In recent years French presidents have attempted to leave their mark on society by commissioning large projects – for example, Georges Pompidou with the Pompidou Centre, (Beaubourg), a futuristic multimedia and exhibition centre in Paris, or François Mitterand with the new Opera Bastille.

To have one's name linked with a cultural achievement is considered the ultimate in personal prestige. Being regarded or referred to as an *intellectuel/le* is a term of praise since high culture is respected by all, whether educated or not.

Légion d'honneur

The *Légion d'honneur*, created by the Emperor Napoleon, is still one of France's greatest honours. It is conferred for services rendered to the nation. People who have received this honour wear a tiny red ribbon in the shape of a rosette in their lapel.

Your health is important and you are safe in France. The French are great consumers of medical services, certainly by British standards. Do not worry unduly if you are sent for an X-ray; they are just checking that your cold has not reached your chest. It will give you the opportunity of viewing the consultant's antiques in the waiting-room. Alternatively, bring your paracetamols along.

The safest and cheapest way is to go to a chemist's (*pharmacie* indicated by a green cross outside). They will suggest sensible solutions in case of minor problems or refer you to a doctor's practice, whose details they will have. Make sure you ask for a *médecin conventionné* who is legally bound to charge you the official rate to be refunded by the *sécurité sociale* (if you are on E101 from Britain). If you have private insurance, go and admire the antiques. In all cases, keep your receipts. You need not be shy about your health as the French love talking about their illnesses, and gory details of surgery are cheerfully swapped at bus stops. And so,

Bonne chance, Bonne santé, Bon appétit, Bon séjour
Bonnes vacances, Bon voyage
&
A la prochaine!

If you have now developed an appetite for reading about the French because they failed to behave in any way this guide tried to warn you about, you may like to delve into the thousands of pages of facts and figures published in *Quid* updated yearly. Did you know for, instance, that the average height of conscripts enlisted in 1939 was 1.66 metres, while it shot to 1.74 m. in 1980. The helpful suggestion is that the introduction of cycling enabled people to mate further afield, ensuring healthier offsprings. Oh là là!

O r you may prefer to try reading the slimmer five hundred-odd pages of *The French*, by Theodore Zeldin, an Englishman who 'knows us better than we know ourselves', or so they say modestly, in such a . . . how shall I put it? – un-French way, maybe!

French Words Used In This Book

à la française 23 — in the French manner
apéritif 40 — before-meal drink taken as an appetizer

Auberges de Jeunesse 65 — Youth Hostels
autoroutes à péage 55 — toll motorways
baptême 30 — baptism, christening
biscotte 38 — toasted bread
boulangerie 41 — baker's shop
Boulevard Périphérique 56 — ring road around Paris & main cities
carnet 59 — booklet of Metro/bus tickets

Cédez le passage 55 — give way (to traffic on roundabout)

Chambre d'hôtes 65 — Bed and Breakfast
charcuterie 41, 44 — cold meats, sausages, etc.

communion solonelle 30 — First Communion
composter 58 — to validate one's rail ticket in a machine

croque monsieur 50 — ham and cheese toasted sandwich

départements 14 — administrative districts
Départements d'outre mer (DOM) 13, 14 — overseas districts
Écoles publiques 70 — state schools
entre la poire et le fromage 46 — interval for lively conversation at the end of a meal

fleuves 15 — major rivers

France métropolitaine *13*	the French homeland
France profonde, la *23*	the countryside ('Deep France')
gens du Nord, les *16*	people of Northern France, as perceived by the South
goûter *40*	afternoon snack
Hexagone, l' *13, 14*	term used for France, because of its shape
Hôtel de Ville *59*	Town Hall
médecin conventionné *73*	medical practitioner in state scheme
mère patrie, la *13*	mother country
mes sentiments dévoués/ les meilleurs *27*	sincere regards/best regards (conventional phrases for ending letters)
Métro, le *59*	the tube, underground railway, subway
métropole, la *13*	mainland France
midi, le *16*	the South of France
Office du Tourisme *64*	Tourist Information Office
papiers *15*	personal documents
petites mains *20*	expert seamstresses in fashion houses
porte cochère *35*	entrance to an apartment building
pourboire *50*	tip, gratuity ('for a drink')
Président Directeur Général (PDG) *52*	managing director

Index